PEOPLE OF CHARACTER

Rosa Parks

A Life of Courage

Written by Tonya Leslie
Illustrated by Tina Walski

BLASTOFF! 4 READERS

BELLWETHER MEDIA · MINNEAPOLIS, MN

Note to Librarians, Teachers, and Parents:

Blastoff! Readers are carefully developed by literacy experts and combine standards-based content with developmentally-appropriate text.

Level 1 provides the most support through repetition of high-frequency words, light text, predictable sentence patterns, and strong visual support.

Level 2 offers early readers a bit more challenge through varied simple sentences, increased text load, and less repetition of high frequency words.

Level 3 advances early-fluent readers toward fluency through increased text and concept load, less reliance on visuals, longer sentences, and more literary language.

Level 4 builds reading stamina by providing more text per page, increased use of punctuation, greater variation in sentence patterns, and increasingly challenging vocabulary.

Level 5 encourages children to move from "learning to read" to "reading to learn" by providing even more text, varied writing styles, and less familiar topics.

Whichever book is right for your reader, Blastoff! Readers are the perfect books to build confidence and encourage a love of reading that will last a lifetime!

This edition first published in 2008 by Bellwether Media.

Library of Congress Cataloging-in-Publication Data
Leslie, Tonya.
  Rosa Parks : a life of courage / by Tonya Leslie.
    p. cm. – (People of character) (Blastoff! readers)
Summary: "People of character explores important character traits through the lives of famous historical figures. Rosa Parks highlights how this great individual demonstrated courage during her life. Intended for grades three through six"–Provided by publisher.
  Includes bibliographical references and index.
  ISBN-13: 978-1-60014-088-4 (hardcover : alk. paper)
  ISBN-10: 1-60014-088-2 (hardcover : alk. paper)
  1. Parks, Rosa, 1913-2005–Juvenile literature. 2. Courage–United States–Juvenile literature. 3. African American women–Alabama–Montgomery–Biography–Juvenile literature. 4. African Americans–Alabama–Montgomery–Biography–Juvenile literature. 5. Civil rights workers–Alabama–Montgomery–Biography–Juvenile literature. 6. African Americans–Civil rights–Alabama–Montgomery–History–20th century–Juvenile literature. 7. Segregation in transportation–Alabama–Montgomery–History–20th century–Juvenile literature. 8. Montgomery (Ala.)–Race relations–Juvenile literature. 9. Montgomery (Ala.)–Biography–Juvenile literature. I. Title.

F334.M753P385525 2008
323.092–dc22
   [B]   2007015013

Contents

What does it mean to have **courage**? Could you be brave in the face of danger? Would you stand up for something that was right?

Rosa Parks did. She showed the world how to be courageous and she did it by sitting down.

Rosa Parks was born in Tuskegee, Alabama in 1913. As a child, Rosa couldn't go to certain schools. She could not shop in some stores. She couldn't eat in certain restaurants. She couldn't do these things because of the color of her skin. Rosa Parks was black.

In 1913, African-American people didn't have the same rights as white people. If you were African-American, you had to ride in a different train car. You had to use a different bathroom. You couldn't even drink from the same water fountain as a white person. Things were separate and definitely not equal. This was called **segregation** and it was the law in some states.

Rosa grew up and became a
seamstress in Montgomery, Alabama.
In her free time, she tried to change
things in her community.

She volunteered and worked with young people. She taught them about equal **rights**. Her work made a difference, but Rosa didn't think things were changing fast enough.

One day, Rosa got on the bus after work. The first four rows of seats were only for white people so Rosa sat behind them. However, she knew that if a white person wanted her seat, she would have to give it up. If she did not, she would be breaking the law.

The bus went from stop to stop. Rosa was tired. She was tired of not having equal rights. She was tired of being **discriminated** against because of the color of her skin. Then a white man got on the bus.

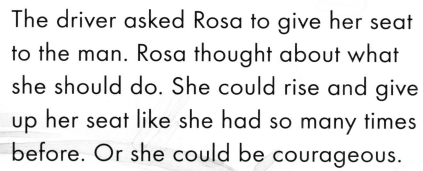

The driver asked Rosa to give her seat to the man. Rosa thought about what she should do. She could rise and give up her seat like she had so many times before. Or she could be courageous.

Rosa decided to take a stand. She told the driver she would not give up her seat. The police came. They told Rosa she was breaking the law. She was arrested. Soon, other people heard about Rosa's act. They thought she was brave. By sitting down, she showed the world that she wasn't going to stand segregation any longer.

Black people began a **boycott**. No one would ride the bus in Montgomery until the discriminating bus laws were changed. It took 381 days to change the laws.

African-Americans around the country heard about Rosa. They decided to stand up against discrimination. Some white people helped too. People marched in **protest**. This was called the **Civil Rights Movement**.

It was a serious time. People fought and struggled to get **equality** for everyone. Rosa got out of jail and continued to protest discrimination. Eventually the laws were changed to give all people equal rights.

After many years, the Civil Rights Movement was a success. Today, people call Rosa the mother of the Civil Rights Movement. She sat down to show the world how to stand up.

Glossary

boycott—when people refuse to buy goods or a service to force a change

Civil Rights Movement—a national effort led by African-American people in the United States in the 1950s and 1960s to establish equal rights

courage—the strength of mind to face danger and difficulties

discrimination—to treat someone differently because of their race, class, or gender

equality—having the same measure or status

protest—to express disapproval

rights—something a person deserves to have

segregation—the forced separation of groups of people according to their race, class, or gender

To Learn More

AT THE LIBRARY

Edwards, Pamela Duncan. *The Bus Ride That Changed History*. Boston, Mass.: Houghton Mifflin, 2005.

Giovanni, Nikki. *Rosa*. New York: Henry Holt & Co, 2005.

Haskins, Jim and Rosa Parks. *I Am Rosa Parks*. New York: Dial Books, 1997.

Ringgold, Faith. *If a Bus Could Talk: The Story of Rosa Parks*. New York: Simon and Schuster, 1999.

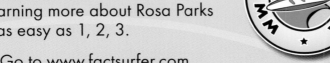

ON THE WEB

Learning more about Rosa Parks is as easy as 1, 2, 3.

1. Go to www.factsurfer.com

2. Enter "Rosa Parks" into search box.

3. Click the "Surf" button and you will see a list of related web sites.

With factsurfer.com, finding more information is just a click away.

Index